# Summary

MW01254257

# The Complete Guide to Fasting
## Dr. Jason Fung

*Conversation Starters*

# By BookHabits

## Tips for Using BookHabits Conversation Starters:

EVERY GOOD BOOK CONTAINS A WORLD FAR DEEPER THAN the surface of its pages. The characters and their world come alive through the words on the pages, yet the characters and its world still live on. Questions herein are designed to bring us beneath the surface of the page and invite us into the world that lives on. These questions can be used to:

- Foster a deeper understanding of the book
- Promote an atmosphere of discussion for groups
- Assist in the study of the book, either individually or corporately
- Explore unseen realms of the book as never seen before

## About Us:

THROUGH YEARS OF EXPERIENCE AND FIELD EXPERTISE, from newspaper featured book clubs to local library chapters, *BookHabits* can bring your book discussion to life. Host your book party as we discuss some of today's most widely read books.

# Table of Contents

# Introducing *The Complete Guide to Fasting*

D r. Jason Fung is a Toronto-based nephrologist whose fasting protocols have been used with over 1,000 patients. His fantastic success has prompted him to create "The Complete Guide to Fasting" with Jimmy Moore, an international bestselling author and veteran health podcaster. Together, they have created a straightforward book offering the background knowledge and tips readers need to consider fasting and implement a successful, healthy fasting plan in their lives. "The Complete Guide to

Fasting" begins with an examination of fasting in a historical sense, answering basic questions many people may have such as the nature of fasting and its practical applications in peoples' diets. Informed by his work as a nephrologist, Dr. Fung provides success stories to motivate readers and prove the effectiveness of fasting as a dietary practice. Aside from describing how fasting may be used for things such as weight loss and Type 2 diabetes, Dr. Fung also answer the question about who should not fast. As the book continues by sections, readers also learn how to fast, resources to use, and recipes to implement. In his section about how to fast, Dr. Fung specifically gives readers a multitude of options, outlining good practices and answering frequently asked questions. In resources, readers find protocol for different types of fasting and a chapter about fluids while fasting. Finally, the authors provide twenty recipes for use in readers' everyday diets- from coffee to wings to salads, there are options for almost any health-conscious individual. "The Complete Guide to Fasting" is written honestly, with personal experience from both Dr. Fung and Jimmy Moore; it features an understanding tone that points out how difficult it is to diet, never mind fast. Its attention to detail and motivational elements help support the authors' viewpoints, allowing for an upbeat and realistic view of fasting and how to implement it as a dietary change for health and weight loss.

"The Complete Guide to Fasting" begins with an introduction by Dr. Jason Fung. He begins by explaining his medical background, touching on his experience with low-fat versus low-carb diets and where his interest in nutrition stemmed from. As Dr. Fung describes his thoughts on different types of dieting, he points out differences in studies concerning the nature of obesity and the factors that cause it. Along with insulin and Type 2 diabetes, the author lists several health issues he studied that were all tied to weight. Dr. Fung's medical experience is offset by Jimmy Moore, who begins his section by describing his experience with Intermittent Fasting. His relaxed and casual writing offer a firsthand perspective on implementing fasting into the average lifestyle, pointing out the practical difficulties and challenges people may face while dieting. Moore makes a point of listing, in detail, the issues he dealt with during his first fast- from caffeine withdrawal symptoms to overeating after the fasting period, Moore explains the common mistakes readers might make without the proper direction and mindset for fasting. As the book continues, readers are given useful knowledge to consider before fasting- the positive effects it has on recognizing the truth of feeling hunger, its possible benefit in cancer prevention and nutritional ketosis. The first section of the book then begins by breaking down the basics of fasting; the authors make a point of explaining how fasting is not starvation- they are completely different, they say, because one is a choice that may be stopped at any time and the other is forced upon you by outside factors. As the authors point out, fasting causes a decrease in insulin, which in turn forces the body to burn stored sugar and body fat. The benefits of fasting can thus be monumental, if done right; it can amount to a full-body cleanse that promotes detoxifying as much as weight loss. "The Complete Guide to Fasting" follows this logic through, using medical information and real-life examples to demonstrate the benefits of fasting and how to safely implement a fast into your lifestyle.

Both prominent voices in the health world, Dr. Jason Fung and Jimmy Moore provide much-needed medical information and motivation for readers considering fasting as a diet option. "The Complete Guide to Fasting" explores both historic and modern examples of fasting, making a case for it as a healthy and sometimes needed alternative to other popular diets. The book follows the format of many diet books, providing success stories and recipes to both motivate and assist readers during their fast. "The Complete Guide to Fasting" is an interesting read, combining medicine and motivation in a positive manner.

# Discussion Questions

*"Get Ready to Enter a New World"*

**Tip:** Begin with questions dealing with broader issues to ensure ample time for quality discussions. Read through all discussion questions before engaging.

## question 1

There is a section at the beginning of the book that features prominent figures who support or implement fasting in their lives. What do you think about these individuals? Does their inclusion give the book authority, or are you still skeptical?

~~~

## question 2

Jimmy Moore gives his personal experience with fasting in the introduction. What is your opinion of his story? Is it motivational or sensational? Why?

~~~

~ ~ ~

# question 3

Dr. Fung refers to a basic principle as supportive of fasting- decreasing insulin leads to burning sugar and body fat. Do you agree with the simple claims he refers to? Why or why not? Do you think it is realistic?

~ ~ ~

~~~

## question 4

There are a few studies and medical research quoted throughout the book. Do these give the book authority, or are you inclined to double-check them for accuracy? Why?

~~~

~~~

## question 5

The authors provide realistic information on both the upsides and downsides to fasting. While it is supposedly healthy and beneficial, they also caution that it can be tough to follow and physically draining. What do you think of the way they describe fasting?

~~~

~~~

## question 6

The novel focuses heavily on fasting as a historical part of diet. Do you agree with the authors' assertions about fasting as having precedent? Why or why not?

~~~

~~~

## question 7

As you read the book, are you able to follow the organization? Why or why not? Is there anything about the layout that does not work for you as a reader?

~~~

~~~

## question 8

There are several recipes provided for readers to use. Do you think these recipes are reasonable? Why or why not? Would you use any of them?

~~~

~~~

## question 9

The authors provide graphs and charts detailing things such as the stages of metabolism. Are these easy to read? Why or why not? Do you think they sufficiently support the claims?

~~~

~~~

## question 10

What do you believe is the most apparent theme or message in the book? Why?

~~~

~~~

## question 11

Do you find that the authors are sufficiently unbiased, or does they make points at any part in the book that seem sensational? If so, give examples and explain.

~~~

~~~

## question 12

Some might point out that fasting is not reasonable for everyone. Do the authors address this? If so, do they do so in an understanding and reasonable manner?

~~~

~~~

## question 13

What do you think about the mental changes that the authors assert could occur due to fasting? Do you believe them or not? Why?

~~~

~~~

## question 14

Are you able to easily determine the risks and benefits of fasting based on the authors' claims? Why or why not? What could they have done to make it better?

~~~

~ ~ ~

## question 15

Much of the novel focuses on the medical evidence the authors believe supports fasting. Do you think you would need to do research individually to confirm, or are the assertions trustworthy?

~ ~ ~

## question 16

"The Complete Guide to Fasting" is not the first book authored by either contributor. Can you tell? Why?

~~~

## question 17

This book focuses on medical support and the practical application of fasting. Does it complete its goal well? Why or why not?

~~~

~~~

## question 18

There are a few success stories in the book. Do you believe them or not? Why? What would you want to change to ensure credibility of the success stories?

~~~

## question 19

Both authors have experience with fasting. Do you think this makes them more credible? Why or why not?

~~~

## question 20

The book is easily divided to allow readers the ability to skip around to different topics. Do you agree with the ordering of the sections? Why or why not?

~~~

# Introducing the Author

D r. Jason Fung is a Canadian nephrologist who has worked in the areas of intermittent fasting and low-carb high-fat dieting. He has specifically studied LCHF and its use in treating individuals with type 2 diabetes. Dr. Fung has implemented a wide range of fasting methods to treat over 1,000 patients; he has had immense success. His medical background and interest in nutrition has made him a world-leading expert in his field.

Jimmy Moore was born December 27, 1971. He obtained a Bachelor of Arts in Political Science and English from the University of Tennessee at Martin and a Master's Degree in Public Policy from Regent University. At one time, Moore was morbidly obese at 410 pounds. He attempted a low-fat diet, which he claims helped him lost weight but ended in him gaining the amount back in only four months. Moore also attempted the Atkins diet, which helped him lose 180 pounds; however, he regained 59 pounds after a span of four years. In 2013, Moore began a self-experiment using a method of ketosis dieting. His incorporation of intermittent fasting and weight lifting also contributed to the experiment. While he has supported the benefits of his weight loss techniques, he does not adhere to the current

American Medical Association's position on cholesterol. Moore has co-authored two books with Associate Professor of Medicine, Dr. Eric C. Westman; the first was titled "Cholesterol Clarity" and the second was titled "Keto Clarity". He has also co-authored "The Ketogenic Cookbook" with Maria Emmerich. He has self-published two books, both of which detail his experience with low-carb dieting.

"The Complete Guide to Fasting" is the first collaboration between Dr. Fung and Moore. Both are prominent figures in the LCHF and fasting communities for their medical expertise and personal experience, respectively. The novels both have worked on received a fair amount of success and positive response from dieting communities. "The Complete Guide to Fasting" is praised as being a comprehensive guide and history of fasting, offering readers the chance to both educate themselves and implement fasting.

"The Complete Guide to Fasting" was published in October 2016. Both authors continue to be active members of the health and diet awareness community, contributing their experiences to many others. The authors' use of medical information and anecdotes continue to influence their writing respectively, making them popular writers in the dieting world. Many lovers of self-help and dieting books received "The Complete Guide to Fasting" with excitement and interest. It ranked #21 overall in Amazon's Diet & Weight loss listing.

# Fireside Questions

*"What would you do?"*

**Tip:** These questions can be a fun exercise as it spurs creativity among the readers by allowing alternate scene endings and "if this was you" questions.

~~~

## question 21

Dr. Fung has extensive experience with fasting methods and how they affect individuals. Do you think this is apparent in the book? How so?

~~~

~~~

## question 22

Moore was at one point morbidly obese. Do you think this fact affects his perspective? How so? Does it make him more or less credible?

~~~

~~~

## question 23

Both of the authors have previously written books. Do you think this is apparent? Why or why not?

~~~

## question 24

Dr. Fung includes several charts, tables, and graphs to illustrate his points about medical information supporting fasting. Why do you think he does this? Are they effective?

~~~

## question 25

Dr. Fung is a medical professional while Jimmy Moore has firsthand experience with fasting. Do you think they are credible sources? Why or why not? Are you inclined to fact-check?

~~~

~~~

## question 26

The book is separated into sections about fasting. Do you agree with this method? Why or why not? How would you structure the book?

~~~

## question 27

If you were writing about this topic, would you have included all of the information that they did? Why or why not? Would you perhaps drop the recipe section in favor of expanding another section? Explain.

~~~

~~~

## question 28

Do the authors use sufficient and unbiased evidence to support their claims? Support your argument.

~~~

~~~

## question 29

Moore has personal experience with fasting and is detailed in his descriptions. Are you inclined to trust him or do you think documentation would make his claims stronger?

~~~

~ ~ ~

## question 30

Can you tell when the different authors contribute (outside of their labeled sections)? How?

~ ~ ~

# Quiz Questions

*"Ready to Announce the Winners?"*

**Tip:** Create a leaderboard and track scores to see who gets the most correct answers. Winners required. Prizes optional.

~~~

## quiz question 1

"The Complete Guide to Fasting" provides both _____ support for intermittent fasting. Dr. Fung and Moore provide these, respectively.

~~~

## quiz question 2

The authors specifically address the difference between _____. One, they explain, is forced while the other is chosen and may be stopped at any time.

~ ~ ~

## quiz question 3

At the beginning of the book, the author explains that fasting forces the body to burn _____. This state is sometimes referred to as 'keto'.

~ ~ ~

~~~

## quiz question 4

**True or False**: The book relies on studies that both Dr. Fung and others have completed. It also uses 'success stories' to illustrate its point.

~~~

~~~

## quiz question 5

**True or False:** While Dr. Fung is an experienced author, Moore is a blogger who does not have academic or practical knowledge of authorship

~~~

~~~

## quiz question 6

**True or False:** The novel is written as both an informative book and a how-to guide. It features recipes and history.

~~~

~~~

## quiz question 7

**True or False:** While Moore has had experience with fasting, he does not describe it as a wonderful and flawless process.

~~~

## quiz question 8

Moore earned a Bachelor's degree in
_____ before earning his
Master's in Public Policy. He eventually became
popular for his experience with fasting and dieting.

~ ~ ~

~~~

## quiz question 9

Dr. Fung is a _____. His experience includes treating type 2 diabetics using fasting methods.

~~~

## quiz question 10

One of the benefits that Moore and Dr. Fung speak consistently about is _____, due to the body burning sugar and fat stores during fasting. This has made fasting popular in recent years.

~~~

## quiz question 11

**True or False:** Moore has only ever tried fasting as a means to lose weight. It was the first method he employed and worked with immense success.

~~~

## quiz question 12

**True or False:** This is not Dr. Fung's first book, although he more commonly publishes in his field and academically.

# Quiz Answers

1. Medical/ancedotal
2. Fasting/starving
3. Sugar/body fat
4. True
5. False
6. True
7. True
8. Political Science/English
9. nephrologist
10. weight loss
11. False
12. True

# Ways to Continue Your Reading

**E**VERY month, our team runs through a wide selection of books to pick the best titles for readers and reading groups, and promotes these titles to our thousands of readers – sometimes with free downloads, sale dates, and additional brochures.

**If you have not yet read the original work or would like to read it again, get the book here.**

# Want to register yourself or a book group? It's free and takes 1-click.

# Register here.

# On the Next Page...

Please write us your reviews! Any length would be fine but we'd appreciate hearing you more! We'd be SO grateful.

**Till next time,**

**BookHabits**

"Loving Books is Actually a Habit"

CPSIA information can be obtained
at www.ICGtesting.com
Printed in the USA
LVHW09s0417191018
594118LV00001B/65/P

9 781389 491238